THE AUSTRALIAN OUTBACK

AND ITS PEOPLE

Kate Darian-Smith and David Lowe

Thomson Learning • New York

PEOPLE
· AND PLACES ·

Cover: A building on the Edjurdina sheep station used when horses drove the sheep.

Title page: Only a few sparse bushes and grasses grow in this desert land.

Contents page: Artist Michael Tommy Tjabarndi paints Aboriginal designs onto a piece of cloth.

First published in the United States in 1995 by
Thomson Learning
115 Fifth Avenue
New York, NY 10003

First published in Great Britain in 1994 by
Wayland (Publishers) Ltd.

Library of Congress Cataloging-in-Publication Data
Darian-Smith, Kate.
    The Australian outback and its people / Kate Darian-Smith and
David Lowe.
        p.   cm.—(People and places)
    Includes bibliographical references and index.
    ISBN 1-56847-337-0
    1. Australian Outback—Juvenile literature. I. Lowe, David. 1964–
II. Title. III Series.
DU96.D37   1995
919.4—dc.20   94-34822

Printed in Italy

Acknowledgments
The publishers would like to thank the following for allowing their photographs to be reproduced in this book:
Australian High Commission: 36; Christine Osborne Pictures: 14 bottom, 16, 17, 29; Eye Ubiquitous: *title page, contents page,* 8, 13 top, 28, 44 (Grenville Turner), 11 top, 31, 37 bottom (Philip Quirk), 11 bottom, 15, 23 (Carolyn Johns), 14 top, 18 (Matthew McKee), 19, 33 right (John Miles), 22, 26 (David Moore), 40 (Jason Busch), 42 (Peter Jarver), 43 top (Bennett Dean); Eye Ubiquitous/TRIP; 39, 43 middle (J. Wakelin); FLPA: 10 (W Wisniewski); Impact Photos Ltd.: 5 top (Richard McCaig), 41 (Nick Dolding); Mary Evans Picture Library: 20; NHPA: 5 bottom (Martin Harvey), 7, 12, 37 middle (Otto Rogge), 9 top, 34, 38 (A.N.T.), 9 middle (Daniel Heuclin), 13 bottom (Ralph and Daphne Keller), 24 (Ford Kristo); Robert Harding Picture Library Limited: 25, 35 (C. Bowman); Sue Passmore: *cover* 6, 30, 32, 45; Topham Picture Source: 27.
Artwork by Peter Bull 4, 21.

CONTENTS

· T H E · S U N B U R N T · C O U N T R Y ·

*I*t is hard to give a definition of the Australian outback, although the term is well known. The outback is generally understood to mean the largely uninhabited and dry regions of inland Australia. The term actually describes more than two-thirds of Australia, the world's driest continent. Australia's areas of fertile soils and tropical vegetation are found only along its coastlines.

Rainfall is low in the outback, so much of this land consists of desert. Only about 15 percent of Australians lives there; the other 85 percent of the population lives in the major cities along the coast. There are few towns or settlements of any size, even along the Stuart Highway, which runs 1,865 miles from Darwin in the north to Adelaide in the south. Alice Springs, with its 23,000 inhabitants, is like an island of people in the middle of Australia.

The small communities of the outback live in a great range of environments, since there are many different ecosystems and habitats stretching across this vast continent. One of the outback's most striking features is the number of contrasts it presents: it is usually so dry that any form of life is a struggle, but it can also be awash with floods during freak rains. Much of the outback consists of flat plains, yet some of the most unusual rock

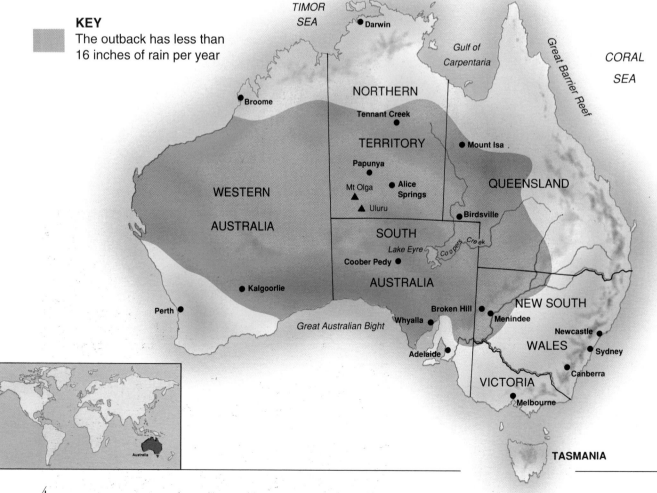

KEY
The outback has less than 16 inches of rain per year

formations in the world can be found there. Unique and beautiful animals and plants attract tourists in large numbers.

The soils of the outback are mostly low in nutrients and are sometimes rust red. This color results from years of erosion and oxidation, a process by which the soil rusts. The center of Australia, the heart of the outback, is often known as the "red center."

These sandstone rocks are over 400 million years old.

The Making of Australia

Australia was originally part of the supercontinent, Gondwanaland, that consisted of most of the lands now south of the equator. Over a long period of time, Gondwanaland broke up into the various continents of today.

Until about 100,000 years ago, ocean levels were low enough for animals and plants to cross the seas between Australia and Southeast Asia. When sea levels rose, Australia was completely separated from other land masses and Australian species of animals and plants were cut off from the rest of the world. This led to the development of animals and plants different from any others.

The Australian landscape changed with different geological periods. When layers of rock and quartz were lifted up and folded during great earth movements, they formed mountain ranges. In central Australia, Mt. Conner, Uluru, and Mt. Olga are the remainders of a mountain range formed in this way. Their rocks are some of the oldest in the world.

Mt. Olga at sunset.

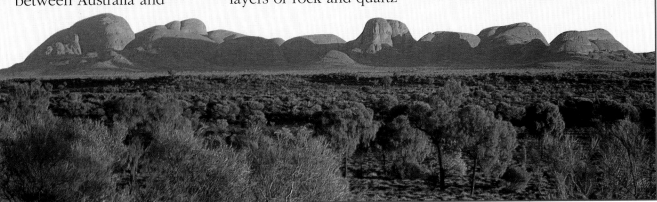

Shearing sheds at an isolated sheep station in the dry interior of Australia.

SURVIVING

The harsh climate affects all forms of life in the outback. The annual rainfall of most of the outback is less than 16 inches. Long droughts are common and there are many tales of the hardships droughts have brought. For example, the drought of 1956-66 was so severe that the Australians began calling the red center the "dead center." During this drought, half the cattle in the outback died.

Where possible, farmers tap basins of underground water to help fight droughts and to provide regular water sources for cattle and sheep. The largest of these underground basins is the Great Artesian Basin, which stretches beneath almost a quarter of the continent. Although the underground waters can be of great help, they cannot prevent some of the effects of a long drought. The loss of animal and plant life and the damage to soil can take years to repair.

Life in the outback also has to survive extreme heat. Heat waves of up to 160 days have been recorded in northwest Australia, and temperatures of 113° F are not uncommon. In contrast, in summer (December through February) it can become very cold at night. Days of 113° F can give way to nights plunging as low as 14° F – a range of 99° F in 12 hours!

The Aboriginal people and other Australians who brave these conditions live in small settlements, isolated homesteads, and the few towns of the outback. Most of these inhabitants are involved in raising cattle for beef or sheep for wool, growing cereal crops (especially wheat), mining in some form, or tourism. These industries are very important, not only to the people of the outback, but also to Australia's economy.

My Country

The poem "My Country" was written in 1908 by nineteen-year-old Dorothea Mackellar. Learned at school by generations of children, it is probably the best known poem in Australia. "My Country" describes the contrasts of the outback.

I love a sunburnt country,
A land of sweeping plains,
Of ragged mountain ranges,
Of droughts and flooding rains.
I love her far horizons,
I love her jewel-sea,
Her beauty and her terror –
The wide brown land for me!

Core of my heart, my country!
Her pitiless blue sky,
When sick at heart, around us,
We see the cattle die –
But then the grey clouds gather,
And we can bless again
The drumming of an army,
The steady, soaking rain.

Shifting sands reveal the skull of a goat in the desolate landscape of the outback.

Given the harsh environment, many visitors are surprised by the variety of life that exists in the outback. Indeed, some of Australia's rarest species of flora and fauna, or plants and animals, have their homes there. Discoveries of fossils are constantly telling us more about the plants and animals that lived there thousands of years ago. Some of the prehistoric animals were larger forms of well-known Australian animals, such as kangaroos and wombats.

Before the Europeans arrived, the only domestic animal in Australia was the dingo, or wild dog. Dingoes were introduced to Australia from Indonesia around 6,000 years ago. Now Australian animals also compete with introduced species such as rabbits, foxes, cats, sheep, and cattle.

Crocodiles have lived in Australia for many thousands of years.

CREATURES OF THE OUTBACK

Marsupials, animals that keep their young in pouches, are found only in Australia, New Guinea, the Moluccas, and the Americas. Marsupials found in the outback include kangaroos, wombats, koalas, possums, wallabies, and numbats. One of the most unusual Australian animals is the echidna, or spiny anteater. The echidna is a mammal – female echidnas provide milk for their young. But the young echidna is born from an egg with a leathery shell. Echidnas adapt well to dry conditions in the outback, eating ants and grubs. They can defend themselves with their sharp spines when they need to.

Smaller creatures also roam the outback, although they are often difficult to find. You could spend days without seeing more than a few lizards and lots of ants and flies. The inland of Australia is particularly rich in insect life.

On the other hand, you could also be unlucky enough to stumble across the eastern taipan, the most venomous snake in the world. Other common venomous snakes are the death adder, the eastern brown snake, and the tiger snake. Most Australian snakes use poison to stun or kill their prey.

Some of the smallest inhabitants of the outback can leave very striking signs of their presence. Termites in northern Australia build large hills which can be six feet high or higher. They are called magnetic termite hills because they are always built to lie north-south. It is thought that this is a means of regulating the temperature of the hills by convection.

The wedge-tailed eagle is one of the largest eagles in the world.

BIRDS

Birds are the most obvious wildlife during the day. Colorful small birds such as finches and budgerigars (also called parakeets) gather near water holes. Galahs – gray and pink cockatoos – flock to areas where trees grow. And the emu, a large, flightless bird like an ostrich, roams widely. The call of the kookaburra sounds like a laugh and is heard all over Australia.

The wedge-tailed eagle is an important part of the outback. Aboriginal drawings tell stories about the eagle's role in shaping the country. Eagle feathers are also used as decoration in the ceremonies of some Aboriginal groups.

Eagles feed on small mammals such as rats, rabbits, and small wallabies. They have adjusted to changes in the types of food available to them. Numbers of native mice, wallabies, and other marsupials have declined since the arrival of the Europeans, so eagles have since turned to eating rabbits and occasionally small lambs. This change in diet causes a problem for those concerned for Australia's environment. If farmers have to reduce the number of rabbits, will the wedge-tailed eagles be able to adjust again and find different food?

NOCTURNAL LIFE

Marsupials are not usually seen during the day, except for the occasional kangaroo resting in the shade of a tree. Kangaroos and most other marsupials are nocturnal, which means they are active mainly at night. As well as the bigger gray and red kangaroos, there are many smaller species. In rocky outcrops near the center of the outback, the yellow-footed rock wallaby might be seen. It has a special method of keeping cool in the heat of the day. It licks its bare arms until there is a good layer of saliva covering them. This then evaporates and draws with it the heat from the blood underneath. The cooled blood can then circulate throughout the wallaby's body.

European settlement has affected the smaller species of kangaroo. Since settlement, 6 of the 48 species of kangaroo have become extinct, and others are endangered. This is because their habitats have been damaged or destroyed by new farming methods and new animals introduced to the outback.

A dingo pup. Dingoes hunt mainly at night – sometimes in groups.

Kangaroos are one kind of marsupial. The first Europeans could hardly believe that such animals, with pouches for their young, existed.

After rains, colorful wildflowers bloom in the Simpson Desert.

After a shower of rain, a bare-looking patch of soil can turn into a field of white Darling lilies. The seeds, activated by the-rain, germinate, flower, seed, and then die – all within ten days.

A number of species of Australia's famous eucalyptus trees, or gum trees, grow in the outback. One small but very hardy species is the dwarf mallee, which is found in many areas. Ghost gums and other eucalypts can survive harsh conditions.

There are few areas in the outback that have no plants. Rolling dunes of sand are found only in a few places, such as the Western Desert. Even here, plants grow among the dunes. The flowering hakea and grevillea plants can create a colorful contrast to the orange sand. Small trees, shrubs, and grasses are scattered throughout the outback. Desert plants have evolved a number of methods of survival. The hummock or spinifex grass has stalks as thin as needles to keep water from evaporating in the heat. Its roots bind the loose soils and sands and prevent the spreading of dunes. Other plants grow very quickly after rain, even after a single storm. When they die, they leave behind seeds in tough shells that can survive the heat until the next rain comes to release them.

A colorful example of this process occurs in the northwest of New South Wales. This area is well known for its stony or bare surfaces and extreme heat. But not all is as it appears.

WHERE IT RAINS FISH!

In central Australia lies one of the world's strangest lakes. Lake Eyre, 3,590 square miles in area, fills only three or four times every century. When it does, it creates a whole new web of life in a very short time. The lake is fed by rivers that are usually dry. After heavy rains, these carry water hundreds of miles into Lake Eyre. They also carry fish. So rapid is the growth of fish from eggs carried along in the rivers, that it has sometimes been said to rain fish! The fish breed quickly once they arrive in Lake Eyre. In turn, the fish attract thousands of birds, which feed on them. Usually, this life cycle is very short. As the scorching sun evaporates the lake's water, the lake becomes so salty that it eventually kills the fish.

▲
Lake Eyre is normally dry. Its surface is so flat that in 1964, race car driver Donald Campbell set a world speed record on its surface.

Floods in 1984-85 filled Lake Eyre with water.
▼

·ABORIGINAL· ·CULTURE· ·BEFORE·1788·

*A*borigines have occupied the Australian continent for over 50,000 years. In 1788, when the British invaded Australia, it is estimated there were between 750,000 and three million Aborigines living in about 650 different groups, or tribes. Each group had its own dialect, political and social system, laws, and territory. Aboriginal people depended on the environment for their daily survival, and the land was essential to their cultural and religious life.

▲
Some Aborigines use face paint for decoration in traditional ceremonies.

◀

Traditional Aboriginal weapons – boomerangs and spears

Aboriginal women near Broome, on the west coast, collect shellfish. Seafood has always been part of the diet of Aboriginal groups living near the coast.

USING THE ENVIRONMENT

Over thousands of years, Aborigines adapted their lifestyles to suit the often harsh environmental conditions. The size of their territories depended on the climate and other environmental factors. Areas of higher rainfall and more fertile soils, which could support more people on less land, had larger populations. In arid regions, smaller populations were scattered over territories stretching for hundreds of miles. The different types of land within Australia meant that there were great differences in Aboriginal lifestyles.

Aborigines lived a seminomadic life, traveling throughout their land in search of food and camping temporarily near water supplies. Their detailed knowledge of their surroundings meant they knew where to find edible plants and animals, and they knew how to prepare them. For example, in extreme droughts the Bindibu people would obtain moisture from a type of frog that stored water in its body and lived deep in the ground. Also, neighboring tribes would share food and water with those suffering from drought.

The Aboriginal diet was varied, but the type and amount of food was determined by the seasons. After the winter rains, plants flowered and bees produced honey. Kangaroos, wallabies, and other game clustered around water holes. During this time of plenty, large numbers of Aborigines from different groups might gather together to share food, trade objects, and hold ceremonies.

Aborigines developed special tools and skills to manage their environment. Tools were constructed from stone, wood, and bone. Digging sticks were used to dig up yams and other plants, to catch snakes, lizards, and small animals, and to open termite mounds. Axes and cutting tools were used to carve and chop wood. Clubs, spears, and boomerangs were the weapons of hunting and fighting. Returning boomerangs were used only in traditional sporting games and for killing birds. Hunting boomerangs, which did not return, were heavier and often beautifully decorated. Spear-throwers, or woomeras, were used to extend the range of spears.

Fish and shellfish were caught with spears, traps, lines and hooks, nets, and even poison. Aboriginal groups living on the coast or near rivers fished from canoes and rafts. Elaborate traps were set for birds and animals. In central Australia, Aborigines made emu traps by placing sharp stakes at the bottom of a large hole, then covering the hole with branches and grass. In the southwestern part of Western Australia, trenches were dug to trap the hind legs of kangaroos.

Grinding stones were used to prepare seeds and nuts for eating. Food preparation sometimes involved removing poisonous substances from plants. Food was stored in containers made from wood, bark, and woven fibers. The environment provided all the materials for the manufacture of clothing, ornaments, medicines, shelter, and goods for trading. Nothing was ever wasted.

Searching for "bush tucker" – natural foods from plants and animals – required everyone's help. In the desert, men would hunt for the larger animals like emus and kangaroos. Women gathered the fruits of desert plants, known today as "bush raisins" and "bush

▲

These seeds are dried, ground into flour with stones, and baked as a type of dough.

◄

An Aboriginal woman prepares food.

tomatoes," and harvested the seeds of grasses. They tracked small marsupials and reptiles and found plump witchetty grubs – large moth larvae that live in the ground and are rich in protein. Young children played games with toy digging sticks and spears. They learned hunting and gathering skills from adults. Because they understood their environment so well, Aboriginal groups needed to spend only about five hours a day, on average, searching for food, and this left them plenty of time for other activities.

FIRE-STICK FARMERS

Aborigines were "fire-stick" farmers. They regularly burned off undergrowth to create and maintain pastures. Ash from the fire fertilized the soil, so that a rich crop of grass would grow after the first rain. Animals were attracted to the pastures and could be hunted more easily. Burning off caused the regeneration of some species like the bush tomato and ensured a steady supply of plant foods. Fire was also used to clear paths for travel.

Aboriginal Languages

Before the European invasion, there were more than 200 different languages spoken throughout Australia. These were as different from one another as Finnish is from Italian. There were also several dialects of each language. Each Aboriginal group spoke its own language or dialect, and people could usually speak the languages of their neighbors.

Europeans forced Aborigines to give up their own languages and speak English instead. Today, only about 50 Aboriginal languages are still the everyday form of communication for large groups. Some of these languages are now used along with English in schools and on television and radio stations that broadcast to Aboriginal communities living in remote areas. Aborigines believe that it is important that these languages remain a living part of Aboriginal cultures.

There are about 20 different sounds in Aboriginal languages, some of which are not used in English. But some Aboriginal words have been absorbed into English. For example, in 1770 Captain Cook recorded some of the language of the Guugu-Yimidhirr people of northern Queensland, including the word *kangooroo* – the kangaroo. Words such as *boomerang* and *dingo* were taken from the Dharuk language spoken in the area around Sydney. Another Aboriginal word that is now an accepted part of Australian English is *billabong*, a combination of *billa*, which means river, and *bong*, which may have meant dead. A billabong can be a pond or a dry river that fills with water only during heavy rain.

Australian children watch Aboriginal dancers perform. The dancers are part of a group that tours schools, telling children about Aboriginal culture.

A cave painting of the Rainbow Serpent in the Northern Territory. The Rainbow Serpent was one of the Ancestral Beings who created the world in the Aboriginal Dreamtime.

ABORIGINAL BELIEFS

In Aboriginal cultures, the visible and invisible sides of life could not be separated. Everyday activities, from collecting food to making tools, had a religious meaning as well as a practical one.

Traditional Aboriginal religious beliefs called the time of creation Dreamtime. In Aboriginal histories, Ancestral Beings traveled across Australia in the Dreamtime. These beings were spirit-creatures who came from the sky, the sea, or under the ground. They created the land and all living things. The Ancestral Beings made valleys, mountains, rivers, plants, animals, and humans. They also gave Aboriginal groups their territories. One Ancestral Being was Kuniya the carpet snake, who camped on a flat sand hill. The sand hill turned to stone and became Uluru (Ayers Rock). Another was the Rainbow Serpent, represented sometimes as a terrifying snake with a kangaroo head and crocodile teeth, and sometimes as a rainbow.

The Ancestral Beings made laws governing the relationships between all forms of life and the land. Aborigines followed these laws. They covered social and political structures, family relationships, and relationships between people and the natural world. Aborigines placed great importance in the care for sacred sites, the places visited by Ancestors during Dreamtime travels. Aboriginal communities that have a semitraditional lifestyle still look after their sacred sites.

Ancestral Beings and other spirits could be called upon through religious rituals, and were active in the lives of people and animals. Preparations for some religious ceremonies lasted for days. Songs were composed and dances were performed. Symbolic paintings were drawn on the ground, on bark, or on rock. Some groups decorated their bodies with ochre and feathers.

Aborigines managed their environment with great success and lived in harmony with their lands. This harmony was destroyed by the arrival of white settlers.

Early white settlers built houses from branches, bark, and mud.

*A*ustralia was used originally by Great Britain as a penal colony. From 1788 on, the first convict ships began to arrive in Australia with their cargoes of prisoners. These were followed by waves of free immigrants. Colonies grew quickly, and cities were built at the main coastal ports. Exploring parties set off inland to make maps and collect scientific information. They were paving the way for animal farmers who would soon run cattle and sheep on grazing lands, for agriculturists who would try to cultivate the land, for traders, and for miners. The new settlers were hungry for land.

By the 1840s, although much of southeastern and southwestern Australia had been surveyed, the interior remained a mystery. It was widely believed that Australia's heart would be fertile, watered by a massive river or inland sea. But explorers found the dry lands difficult to enter because there were few rivers or water holes. The Aborigines, who understood the land, were not usually asked about the best routes for traveling. In fact, they were often murdered by explorers. When Aborigines did help explorers, their services usually went unrecognized.

By 1858 only the driest lands in central, west, and northwest Australia were still unexplored by Europeans. John McDouall Stuart and his party reached the center in 1860. Further surveying of the outback proved that no inland sea existed.

Burke and Wills's Expedition

On August 21, 1860, an expedition led by Robert O'Hara Burke and his second-in-command, George Landells, left Melbourne to attempt to cross the continent from south to north. The expedition was lavishly equipped with 18 men, dozens of camels, horses, and wagons, tons of firewood, and enough food for two years. Burke was in such a hurry that he abandoned most of the equipment – and was abandoned by Landells – in Menindee. Burke went ahead with a small party to Cooper Creek. Telling the others to wait there, he headed north with his new second-in-command, William John Wills, two men named Gray and King, some camels, and provisions for 12 weeks. It was the wet season in the desert, and the camels got bogged down and died. But all four men reached the Gulf of Carpentaria to complete the first north-south crossing by Europeans. Gray died of illness a few weeks into the return trip. Burke, Wills, and King were starving.

They finally reached Cooper Creek, exhausted and near death, to find that the camp had been abandoned only hours before. When local Aborigines offered food, Burke shot at them. Burke and Wills perished, but King survived because he accepted help from the Aborigines.

These expeditions were dangerous and difficult. Many people died exploring Australia. ▶

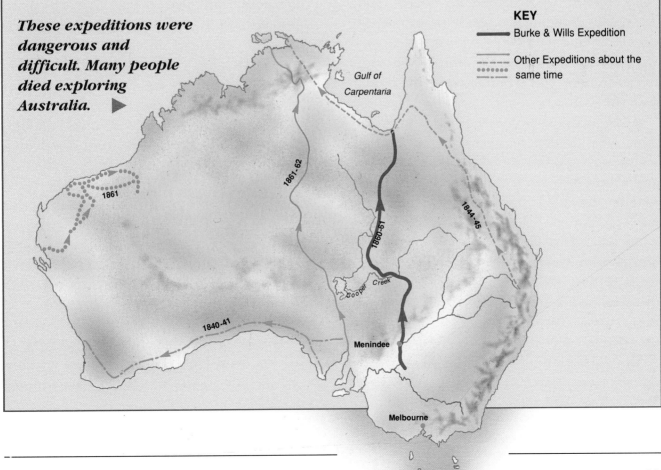

KEY
— Burke & Wills Expedition
‑ ‑ ‑ Other Expeditions about the
•••• same time

Gulf of Carpentaria

1861-62

1861

1860-61

1844-45

1840-41

Cooper Creek

Menindee

Melbourne

Mission housing for Aborigines, such as this at the Santa Teresa Mission, was often inadequate.

TERRA NULLIUS

When the British took possession of Australia, they claimed it was *terra nullius* (unoccupied). They signed no treaties with Aboriginal groups nor offered any compensation for taking their lands. At first, Aborigines welcomed and assisted the British. But soon white settlers and Aborigines were at war over the land.

Aboriginal spears were no match for European guns. Settlers massacred entire Aboriginal groups and kidnapped Aboriginal women and children to work as servants. The white settlers defended their violent actions by arguing that Aboriginal peoples and cultures were inferior to European peoples and cultures – they were considered nonpeople. As well as this, the introduction of European diseases had a terrible effect on Aboriginal populations. By 1901, their numbers had dropped to only 50,000.

Driven from their own lands, many Aborigines were forced to live on government reservations and missions. Others had no choice but to work for the Europeans. Colonial and, later, state governments controlled their lives with policies that aimed to make Aborigines fit into white society. By the early twentieth century, Aboriginal populations were beginning to increase, but their freedom of movement was restricted and they were kept apart from other Australians.

On a number of outback cattle stations, 80 percent of the workers were Aborigines. Sometimes they received only rations in return for their labor. In 1946, Aboriginal workers in Western Australia went on strike in protest at their low pay and working conditions. In 1966, Aborigines walked off cattle stations in the Northern Territory and began a struggle to obtain the ownership of their land, which was finally to be successful.

In 1967 Aborigines were given the status of citizens. They demanded recognition of their traditional land rights, control of their communities, and a say in government decisions.

LAND USE

The colonial governments gave, sold, and leased land to settlers. Settlers chopped down forests and cleared scrubland with axes and with machines like the stump-jump plow, a unique invention that lifted itself over obstacles. While European farming methods were unsuitable for Australian soils and climates at first, these were adapted to the environment over time. More recently, bulldozers have been used in farming.

Intensive agriculture makes up only about 10 percent of land use in Australia and is concentrated in the fertile areas along the east coast. About two-thirds of the country is used for grazing sheep and cattle on natural pasture. Cattle are mainly in the drier central and northern areas, while sheep are found in the southwest and southeast. There are about 160 million sheep in Australia. They are often grazed alongside wheat-growing areas in what is known as the sheep-wheat belt. Wool has been an important export since the 1820s; Australia is the world's largest producer of wool. Australia also exports half of the beef it produces.

Wheat is Australia's most important crop. Recently, better farming methods and new types of wheat have increased the amount of wheat produced and exported.

THE DROVER

Stock routes were established in the nineteenth century to move cattle into new lands and out to markets. It could take months to walk the vast herds across, or up and down, the continent. This work was known as droving. In the late nineteenth century, the lives of drovers, shearers, shepherds, and other bush workers were romantically portrayed by writers and artists who were trying to create a sense of national pride in Australia.

The Ballad of the Drover (Henry Lawson 1889)

Across the stony ridges,
Across the rolling plain,
Young Harry Dale, the drover,
Comes riding home again.
And well his stock horse bears him
And light of heart is he,
And stoutly his old pack horse
Is trotting by his knee.

Up Queensland way with cattle,
He travelled regions fast;
And many months have vanished,
Since homefolk saw him last.
He hums a song of someone
He hopes to marry soon;
And hobble chains and camp-ware
Keep jingling to the tune.

▲
Today, motorcycles as well as horses are used to herd cattle.

·MINING·AND·
·TECHNOLOGY·

▲
Trucks spray liquid to wet down dangerous dust from uranium mines.

The Australian continent is rich in mineral resources. The outback has been drilled for oil and gas, but these are not its richest prizes. In recent years, Australia has been the world's biggest producer of bauxite, the substance from which aluminum is made. Australia has been one of the largest producers of gold, coal, iron ore, and uranium. Uranium is used in nuclear power plants to generate electricity and to make nuclear weapons. Mining uranium in Australia has been controversial. At the moment only a fraction of it is mined.

Because minerals contribute around 25 percent of Australia's income from exports, the mining industry is very important. Most of the mining takes place in remote areas. Much of the ore is exported overseas. Some is processed in Australian towns, such as Whyalla in South Australia and Newcastle in New South Wales, where steel is made. But the percentage of ores processed in Australia is still low. If Australia can process more of its raw material and sell more finished goods, it will not have to depend so much on the price of its ore, which can go up and down.

PRECIOUS METALS

The search for precious metals led many thousands of pioneering white Australians away from the coastline and into the outback. Aboriginal people who stood in the path of the miners searching for minerals were driven out. Mining operations transformed the local environment, ruining the habitats of wildlife and plants: land was cleared, holes were dug, chemicals polluted the soil and water.

GOLD MINING IN KALGOORLIE

Gold was discovered in Australia in the 1850s, and the great gold rushes that followed resulted in huge increases in Australia's population. The population of the Australian colonies was less than half a million in 1851, but nearly four million 50 years later.

In 1893, gold was found in Kalgoorlie in Western Australia. Most of the gold near the surface was mined very quickly. Deep mines had to be sunk to bring more gold nuggets out of the ground.

Gold mining continues today in Kalgoorlie. The huge numbers of men with picks and shovels and the camels and horses that carried goods and gold are gone now. In their place are large rock-crushing machines, conveyor belts, and acids to help separate the gold from other materials. Trucks, roads, and railroads support the town's activities.

Many gold-mining towns have suffered a decline, either because the gold has run out or because there has been a fall in the price of gold. Kalgoorlie – a busy, bustling place with a population of 20,000 – has been more fortunate, because it has more than just gold to mine. It also has vast resources of nickel, which is often used to harden steels. When the price of gold dropped during the 1960s and 1970s, more nickel was mined. Since the early 1980s, when gold prices started to rise again, gold mining in Kalgoorlie has resumed on a large scale.

The main street in Kalgoorlie, where mining continues today

An aerial view of the Mount Isa mining complex

In early times, it was difficult to live in mining towns such as Mount Isa in northwestern Queensland. Today, a lifestyle involving hot, dusty, and remote environments and mining above or beneath the ground still might not be regarded as easy, but the town has grown and changed to help its inhabitants.

The mining industry in Mount Isa supports a population of over 25,000 in a cleaner environment than that of many mining towns in Europe. With an average of only five cloudy days per year, the waste burned in the mine's chimneys escapes more easily into the atmosphere. But concerns remain about the long-term impact of mining on the surrounding environment.

An American-owned company, Mount Isa Mines Limited, runs the mine and has a mixed record with its workers. In the middle of the 1960s, a dispute over workers' wages led to violence, and the company fired many workers. Since then, however, Mount Isa Mines has played a more positive role in making workers' environments more comfortable. The company has helped to build new "outback suburbs," providing health clubs and other services. A big water sports festival is held every year on a lake at the edge of the town. Living conditions overall are greatly improved since the 1960s.

ATOMIC TESTING

The vast area of flat, dry, and almost uninhabited land in the outback has long been popular with scientists. Over the last 50 years they have used it as a huge open-air laboratory.

Much of central Australia is remote enough to allow secrecy when needed. But secret weapons testing has caused diagreements and serious environmental problems.

In the 1950s, Australia allowed Great Britain to test rockets and atomic bombs in remote secret sites in the outback. The Australian government hoped to share in Britain's knowledge of weapons and technology. But some of these tests were later criticized because of the harm they did to the environment and to the Aboriginal people who lived in the area. An official legal inquiry into 12 atomic bombs exploded by the British in the 1950s was held in the 1980s. It concentrated on the radioactive fallout, or poisonous dust that is created when atomic bombs explode. The inquiry reported that fallout had contaminated test sites and areas where Aboriginal groups lived. Recently, the British government agreed to provide $30 million to workers and Aboriginal groups as compensation. Much of the contaminated area will be fenced off for years. The issue still creates arguments in Australia.

The second British atomic
explosion, at Woomera
in 1953

SECRET TECHNOLOGY

Some of the most secret technology in Australia was set up in remote parts of the outback. In the early 1960s, the Australian government signed an agreement with the United States allowing them to build listening and tracking stations in Australia. These stations still operate today. They use special electronic equipment to trace the movements of submarines and to listen for military signals in other countries. Many Australians are unhappy about such stations. They argue that these stations make Australia a target for nuclear attack. There are also people who question whether it is right to have this kind of U.S.-run installation on Australian soil.

·LIFE·IN·THE·OUTBACK·

Today, "road trains" such as this carry goods across the outback.

*P*eople in the outback struggle against a harsh climate and environment and against their isolation from the cities on Australia's coast.

There is still a lot of physical work maintaining fences and securing water. Some Aboriginal communities live in outback towns or run cattle or sheep stations, while others still lead a semitraditional life. But new technologies are quickly changing life in the outback. Although rail lines link the coast with the more remote towns like Alice Springs and Kalgoorlie, some lines have been closed in recent years where road transportation is cheaper. Nowadays, the sight of road trains is common in central Australia.

THE SUN

Many Australians suffer from skin cancer caused by too much exposure to the sun. Skin cancer can be deadly. Public health campaigns warn Australians to protect themselves from the radiation by wearing hats and using sun creams. The sun can also cause people to dehydrate. Unless people avoid the heat of the day or carry a lot of water, they can be in real danger. Many people have gotten lost in the outback without enough water and died.

But the heat of the sun can be put to good use, too. Solar energy is used to generate electricity, provide hot water, and supply power for machines. There are even telephones that work with solar power.

The Capital of the Center

Alice Springs, often called "The Capital of the Center," began as a tiny station on the Overland Telegraph Line linking Adelaide to Darwin. Alice Springs is now an important town for white and Aboriginal communities in the region.

In recent years, the town has become a major tourist center for Australian and overseas tourists who want to visit the outback and the natural beauty of Uluru (Ayers Rock), 265 miles southwest of Alice Springs.

In 1985 the Australian government recognized the Aboriginal ownership of Uluru and the land around it. Aboriginal people now share in managing the booming tourism in the area. Some work as rangers or have other occupations in the national park. Every year roughly 300,000 tourists visit this national park. There is an airport and luxurious tourist accommodation in the middle of the outback at Uluru.

▲ *Tourists watch an Aboriginal performance in Alice Springs. Aborigines own land around Alice Springs and earn some money from tourism.*

Shearing Sheep

Sheepshearing has been one of the most important activities in the outback since European settlement. Shearing appears in famous Australian paintings and stories. Some even say that Australia's best-known song, "Waltzing Matilda," is based on a big shearers' strike in the 1890s.

Today, shearing continues on a larger scale than before. In the northwest corner of New South Wales stands a shearing shed said to be the largest in the world. The Reola Station's shed is three stories high and has pens outside which can hold 2,000 sheep. To herd the sheep, a dozen stock workers use six motorcycles, several four-wheel drive vehicles, one helicopter, and one smaller gyrocopter. Together they cover the station's 988,400 acres and drive the sheep to the pens. In full operation, 16 shearers working inside the shed can remove the fleeces of about 25,000 sheep in just 10 days.

Shearing is the busiest time of the year for these stock workers. At other times, they repair fences, tend sick sheep, and try to ensure that there is enough food for the animals.

Roaming isolated and dry country can be lonely and tiring work, and good radio equipment reduces the sense of loneliness. Modern telecommunication even provides the opportunity for a long-distance college education. Workers often travel great distances to the nearest town, where they can relax and spend some of the money they earn.

Mechanized sheepshearing has now replaced shearing with blades. Sheep farming is an important industry in the outback.

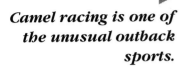

Camel racing is one of the unusual outback sports.

SPORTS

Unusual sports take place at Alice Springs. Every August a strange boat race is held. The "Henley-on-Todd Regatta" is held on the dry bed of the Todd River. Instead of boats, the contestants use craft made from cans. The bottomless boats are carried by contestants, who run the length of the course. A camel race is also held in August.

Birdsville, a tiny settlement of 30 people in Queensland, swells in size each year when several thousand people and horses come from thousands of miles away, by road and by air, to attend a famous horse race.

ART

Many artists and photographers are attracted to the outback by its spectacular changing light, the beautiful colors of the vegetation, and rock formations.

Aboriginal artists, too, have become famous for their paintings of the Australian environment. Albert Namatjira, who lived at the Hermannsburg Mission to the southwest of Alice Springs, used European watercolor techniques in his paintings of the landscapes of the interior. Namatjira was the best-selling artist in Australia during the 1940s and 1950s. Aboriginal artists at Hermannsburg continue to make and sell their artwork today.

Many Aboriginal artists have drawn upon and adapted traditional methods to produce work that is now displayed in major art galleries around the world. In the 1970s, Aboriginal people living in Papunya in the western desert developed their own special school of art. The people of Papunya painted in traditional styles, but used brushes, paints, and boards. They sold their paintings to art galleries and formed their own company. The commercial success of the Papunya art group encouraged other Aboriginal communities to produce and sell their paintings and carvings to tourists and art dealers.

COPING WITH HEAT

Coober Pedy, the oldest and largest opal mining town, is an amazing sight. The name comes from the Aboriginal term meaning "white man's hole in the ground" because the town has very few buildings above ground. Instead, residents live in houses underground.

There are even stores and hotels underground. These underground houses are like normal houses – they often have many rooms and are fully equipped with running water and electricity. Living underground is the best form of protection from the ferocious heat.

White mounds of waste from Coober Pedy mines on flat, red land. The settlement's underground homes protect residents from the heat.

▼

▲

A windowless but cool bedroom of an underground home

ISOLATION

The isolation of the settlements has led to the development of special services. The School of the Air uses radios to teach children in remote areas. The Flying Doctor Service is a medical service that uses radios and aircraft. Founded in 1928 by a missionary and minister, John Flynn, today there are 14 Flying Doctor centers providing medical services throughout the outback.

People living far from hospitals must be prepared to treat common illnesses and dangers such as bites from venomous snakes, broken limbs, or heat exhaustion themselves.

·ENVIRONMENTAL·PROBLEMS·

The outback is prone to such natural disasters as bushfires, floods, and droughts. Other recent ecological disasters are manmade. Just two hundred years of European-style land use and management have resulted in serious environmental problems.

Feral donkeys compete with native animals and livestock for food. The ancestors of these donkeys must have escaped from captivity to the freedom of the outback.

ACCLIMATIZED SPECIES

Today at least 10 percent of Australia's plant life and animals are acclimatized, or introduced species. White settlers deliberately introduced hundreds of species of fish, mammals, plants, and birds. They did this mainly for economic reasons, but also for decorative and sporting purposes. Foxes and mallard ducks were released so that settlers could hunt them for sport. Some domesticated animals such as cats, dogs, goats, camels, horses, and pigs have become feral, or wild.

Introduced flora often compete with and take over from native plants, increase the salinity, or level of salt, in the soil, spread diseases, and disturb the local ecosystem. Several species have become weeds and are kept down with pesticides or biological controls. For example, the cinnabar moth was released to limit the spread of the prickly pear cactus, itself an introduced species. Ranchers are divided about whether acclimatized plants are pests or are useful as food for livestock. One such plant is called both

A prickly pear, one of the plants introduced by European settlers. By 1925, the prickly pear had covered more than 50 million acres, 30 million of which were crop or grazing land. It replaced plants native to Australia. Scientists got the cacti under control when they introduced the cinnabar moth. The caterpillar of this moth is a natural predator of the prickly pear.

Paterson's Curse and Salvation Jane!

With no natural checks like predators or diseases, the populations of some acclimatized species have grown. Livestock, such as cattle and sheep, and feral donkeys, camels, and horses compete for food with native animals and disturb natural food chains. The lives of the smaller animals, such as bilbies and numbats, are threatened as these animals overgraze the land. Some species already face extinction. In addition, the impact of hooves on the ground has led to soil erosion.

Farmers are concerned because some acclimatized feral animals attack livestock and damage fences and farm property. Feral pigs are a menace to both native wildlife and the pastoral and agricultural industries. They eat crops and pastures and prey on lambs. They also eat native animals and wreck the nesting sites of birds. Foxes and feral cats likewise eat native birds, small marsupials, and lambs.

▲
Rabbits at a water hole during a drought.

Rabbits were first brought to Australia in 1859. Of all the acclimatized species, the small European rabbit has had the most disastrous effect on the environment and on farming industries. Female rabbits produce four to six litters a year, each with around six babies. Fifty years after their arrival, millions of rabbits had spread over the continent.

In areas already overgrazed by livestock, the rabbits ate so much vegetation that they turned the land into a semidesert. Native animals and livestock starved to death. Barren land was abandoned.

To solve the problem, rabbits were killed with traps, poison, and guns. Wire mesh fences thousands of miles long were built to stop the "gray tide" of rabbits from spreading into Queensland and Western Australia. They still got through. In the 1950s a virus called myxomatosis, which is fatal to rabbits, was introduced with some success. But rabbits gradually became immune to myxomatosis, so scientists are now developing viruses to make them infertile.

NATIVE PESTS

Europeans regarded dingoes as pests because they attacked livestock. Governments paid large sums of money in bounties to encourage people to trap, shoot, and poison them. In the 1920s, dingo-proof fences were erected through the outback to protect pastures. The fences are over six feet high and run for nearly 62,000 miles through South Australia, New South Wales, and Queensland. The fences have kept dingoes away from sheep properties in southeastern Australia, but there is still a bounty for dingo skins in parts of the outback.

In some areas, the large red, western gray, and eastern gray kangaroo are considered a problem. The clearing of land and stablized water supplies may have helped their numbers to increase. They compete with cattle and sheep for grazing food. Populations of kangaroos are culled, or selectively killed, at regular intervals under the supervision of wildlife authorities, but this practice is opposed by conservation groups. In 1992, more than five million kangaroos were killed. Kangaroo meat is mainly sold for pet food, but has become popular in city restaurants.

The longest fence in the world, built to keep dingoes off property.

Kangaroo meat is eaten by many Australians.

The bilby comes out at night to feed. Today there are only a few bilbies, although they were once common.

ENDANGERED SPECIES

Since white settlement, at least 97 species of plants, 10 species of birds, and 20 species of mammals have become extinct in Australia. Many native plants, birds, and animals in the outback are now in danger of extinction.

The bilby, or rabbit-eared bandicoot, which lives in underground burrows, is one of these endangered species. Once common over half the continent, only small bilby populations survive today. The bilby's natural habitat has been damaged by the overgrazing of livestock, and it competes with rabbits for food and places to build burrows. It is eaten by foxes, dingoes, and feral cats. Unless these factors are controlled, the bilby may disappear completely. Other endangered species share a similar fate.

PROBLEMS WITH THE SOIL

People in the Australian outback face real problems when trying to grow crops. The soil of the outback is shallow and not very fertile. A combination of overgrazing, intensive farming, and the use of pesticides and fertilizers has made the soil even less fertile.

Erosion is another reason for poor soil. Rainfall washes away the thin layer of topsoil year after year, leaving the soil unsuitable for farming and often not even suitable for grazing. Wind can blow away topsoil when there are no plants to hold it down. On top of all this, salt often builds up in the soil – a process called salinization – and nothing at all can grow in it.

·THE·FUTURE·

The communities of the outback have seen many changes in the 1990s. Markets and prices for primary and mineral resources have become less sure. Farmers have had to cope with several bad seasons. Some towns in the sheep-wheat belt are struggling to survive as people move away to the cities. But the people of mining towns such as Broken Hill are determined to maintain their lives in the outback. Other towns, such as Alice Springs, are steadily increasing as tourism and improved transportation bring more and more visitors every year.

Today there are about 270,000 Aborigines in Australia. Three-quarters of these live in the rural towns and lands of the outback. Aboriginal communities still do not have adequate health care, housing, or education. Although governments have started to address these problems, Aborigines have to fight racist attitudes and face problems that white Australians do not have.

A school in an Aboriginal community. Both English and Aboriginal languages are taught.

NATIVE TITLE

During the 1970s and 1980s, laws were passed giving some Aboriginal people back their lands and some control over land use around sacred sites. By 1988 Aborigines owned 10 percent of the continent, mostly land in remote places. But mining companies, who object to having any controls placed on them, remain opposed to many Aboriginal land rights claims.

In 1992 a High Court decision, known as the Mabo judgment, ruled that Australia was not *terra nullius*, or unoccupied, before the British arrived in 1788. This judgment recognizes the Aborigines' rights to traditional lands, or what is known as native title, provided they could show they had a close and continuing relationship with that land.

The Mabo decision was followed by the Native Title Act in 1993. The legislation aims to balance the competing interests of Aborigines, miners, and farmers. It will also compensate those Aborigines who have no "continuing relationship" with their land because they were driven out of it by white settlers. Again, mining companies are opposed, but compromises are being reached.

NEW MEASURES

Both the government and environmental researchers are trying to save national ecosystems before they disappear. Feral animals are being culled, or killed, and scientists continue to develop methods of biological control of acclimatized species such as rabbits.

There have also been tighter measures to stop the smuggling of rare native birds, like parrots and cockatoos, and small animals out of Australia. These birds and animals are drugged, then wrapped in tubes that are placed in false-bottomed suitcases or hidden in the clothes of smugglers. If the creatures survive the journey, they are sold outside Australia for very high prices.

◄ *Rainbow lorikeets are sometimes smuggled abroad, despite being an endangered Australian species.*

A Decade of Land Care

Some landscapes, such as this one, are now being protected from developers.

Preserves and national parks are "safe" areas for native plants and animals. The amount of land in Australia set aside for this purpose has increased. Pastoral properties have been bought by the government and turned into national parks. In addition, the Save the Bush program was set up by the Australian National Parks and Wildlife Service to protect natural habitats that exist outside national parks and other nature preserves.

The 1990s have officially been called a Decade of **Landcare.** People know that trees and other vegetation improve the land, because they protect the soil, offer shelter, and help stop salinization. A project called Greening Australia has planted more than one billion new trees. Heritage conservation will continue to be an important issue for many years.

NEW THINKING ABOUT THE LAND

The Australian government is officially committed to developing the country's land, water, and environmental resources in an environmentally friendly way. One aim is to study, and even reverse, some of the results of land degradation. Cooperative programs among federal and state governments, conservationists, and farmers are working to prevent any more destruction of the environment. Attitudes toward land use are changing, and farmers are taking up new practices.

Solar power makes cheap and clean electricity. Parts of Australia use the sun for their electricity.

▼

ALTERNATIVE ENERGY AND NEW TECHNOLOGY

Although Australia has massive reserves of coal, governments have given a lot of importance to energy that can be renewed. There are plans to construct a solar power plant to provide electricity for the town of Tennant Creek in the Northern Territory. The World Solar Challenge, a solar-car race from Darwin to Adelaide, is an exciting international event and an important way to test new technology.

Australian research in alternative energy is well known internationally, and solar technology that has been developed in the outback is now being sold to the rest of the world.

Many tourists climb the 1,100 feet to the top of Uluru.

Tourists waiting to photograph Uluru at sunset.

TOURISM

Tourism in Australia has grown dramatically since the 1980s. Around three million overseas visitors arrive every year and, at present, the tourist industry employs about 6 percent of the national work force. It accounts for at least 10 percent of Australia's total income. Everyone expects this figure to increase rapidly over the next decade or so.

Tourists come to Australia from all over the world to visit its national parks and World Heritage areas. Unfortunately, tourists can also have bad effects on areas of natural beauty and on national parks. These include damage caused by four-wheel drive vehicles, clearing of vegetation for shelters and campsites, litter left by visitors, and disruption to wildlife. Tourist management of the future must be aware of these things.

Some national parks are now managed by Aboriginal communities. Aborigines are becoming more and more involved in conservation and management plans to protect their own areas, including their outdoor art galleries and sacred sites. Sacred sites have sometimes been placed off-limits to all non-Aboriginals.

THE FUTURE OF THE OUTBACK

Throughout the outback, Aboriginal communities are taking charge of their own lives. Education is improving and prospects are better. Some communities have established businesses in the tourist and pastoral industries. Their future now seems brighter than it has ever been since the first white settlements of 1788.

But the future of the outback and of Australia is tied to world changes. It is predicted that the increasing levels of human-made greenhouse gases and the thinning of the ozone level in the atmosphere will cause world climates to change. These changes will alter the rainfall level over much of Australia, bringing either flooding or a shortage of water. We can only guess at the consequences for the outback, its communities, and its wildlife.

▲
Cooperation on horseback. Aborigines and whites ride together.

▶
King's Canyon, a popular tourist spot between Alice Springs and Uluru.

GLOSSARY

Acclimatized species
A species not native to an area which successfully relocates.

Arid   Dry (land or climate) with an annual rainfall of less than 10 inches.

Artesian Basin   A reservoir of water under the earth's surface.

Biological control   Pest control that involves the introduction of a species into the environment of a pest to destroy that pest.

Conservation   The management of natural resources in a way that will benefit us now and in the future.

Contaminated   Polluted with an unwanted substance.

Convection   A method of transfering heat. As air is warmed, it rises and is replaced by cooler air, which is heavier and sinks.

Cull   To destroy part of a population without affecting the whole population.

Degradation   A change in an environment that makes it less able to support a natural ecosystem.

Dehydrate   To lose water from the body.

Dialect   A variation in words and pronunciation from a standard language.

Ecology   Relation of living things to one another and to their physical surroundings.

Ecosystem   The interaction between a living community and the nonliving environment.

Endangered species
Those likely to become extinct unless action is taken to remove factors threatening their survival.

Erosion   The wearing away of a substance such as soil.

Evaporate   To lose moisture as vapor.

Fauna   All animals of a given time or place.

Federal government
The central government having power over all Australia.

Feral   Describing a domesticated animal that has gone wild.

Flora   All plants of a given time or place.

Germinate   To begin to develop and grow.

Habitat   The environment in which an animal or plant lives.

Intensive farming
Farming that increases production using technology.

Legislation   Laws.

Mammals   A class of animals in which the females suckle their young.

Marsupials   A class of animals in which the females carry their young in pouches until fully developed.

Native   Belonging to the natural flora and fauna of the region.

Ochre   A pigment used to make yellow or red paint.

Oxidation   The process of combining oxygen with a substance, often causing rust.

Ozone level   The level of a gas in the atmosphere that absorbs harmful radiation from the sun.

Pastoral land   Land used for grazing sheep and cattle.

Salinization   The process by which salt builds up in a substance such as water or soil.

Salinity   The level of salt in a substance such as water or soil.

Solar power   Energy from the sun.

BOOKS·TO·READ

Australian Aboriginal Culture. Third edition. New York: Australian Government Publishing Company, 1992.

Baker, Lucy. *Life in the Deserts*. Life In. New York: Franklin Watts, 1990.

Department of Geography Staff. *Australia in Pictures*. Visual Geography. Minneapolis: Lerner Publications, 1990.

Harris, Colin. *Protecting the Planet*. Young Geographer. New York: Thomson Learning, 1993.

Morris, Scott, ed. *Industry of the World*. New York: Chelsea House, 1993.

Nile, Richard. *Australian Aborigines*. Threatened Cultures. Milwaukee: Raintree Steck-Vaughn, 1992.

Rajendra, Vijeya. *Australia*. Cultures of the World. North Bellmore, NY: Marshall Cavendish, 1991.

Reynolds, J. *Down Under: Vanishing Cultures*. San Diego: Harcourt Brace, 1992.

·USEFUL·ADDRESSES·

Australian Government Publishing Company
P.O. Box 7
Planetarium Station
New York, NY 10024

The Australian Institute of Aboriginal and Torres Strait Islander Studies
P.O. Box 553
Canberra ACT 2601
Australia

Environmental Defense Fund
1616 P Street NW
Suite 150
Washington, DC 200036

Friends of the Earth (U.S.A.)
218 D Street SE
Washington, D.C. 20003

Greenpeace U.S.A.
1436 U Street NW
Washington, DC 20009

Office of the Prime Minister of Australia
Parliament House
Canberra, ACT
Australia

INDEX

Numbers in **bold** refer to pictures as well as text.